The
MARCH ON
WASHINGTON

A DAY THAT CHANGED AMERICA

by Margeaux Weston

CAPSTONE PRESS
a capstone imprint

Capstone Captivate is published by Capstone Press, an imprint of Capstone.
1710 Roe Crest Drive, North Mankato, Minnesota 56003
www.capstonepub.com

Library of Congress Cataloging-in-Publication Data is available on the Library of Congress website.
ISBN: 978-1-6639-0587-1 (hardcover)
ISBN: 978-1-6639-2081-2 (paperback)
ISBN: 978-1-6639-0584-0 (ebook PDF)

Summary: Young readers learn about the March on Washington, including what led up to the historic demonstration, how it unfolded, and the ways in which it changed America forever.

Image Credits
Associated Press: cover, 12, Bill Hudson, 13, Charles Gorry, 11; John F. Kennedy Presidential Library and Museum: 14–15; LBJ Library Photo by Cecil Stoughton: 25; Library of Congress: 8, Carl Van Vechten, 21, Charles Alston, 19, Jack Delano, 6, Marion S. Trikosko, 26, Thomas O'Halloran, 24, Warren K. Leffler, 17, 18, 20; Newscom: akg-images, 10, Everett Collection, 7, 9, UPI Photo Service, 5, 22; Shutterstock: Atoly (design element), cover and throughout, TJ Brown, 27

Editorial Credits
Editor: Kristy Stark; Media Researcher: Svetlana Zhurkin; Production Specialist: Kathy McColley

Consultant Credits
Marvin Dulaney, Associate Professor of History Emeritus, University of Texas, Arlington

All internet sites appearing in back matter were available and accurate when this book was sent to press.

Printed and bound in the United States of America.   PO4270

TABLE OF CONTENTS

Words in **bold** are in the glossary.

On August 28, 1963, nearly 250,000 people marched toward the Lincoln Memorial in Washington, D.C. People from across the nation walked together. They marched to send a message of hope and freedom. After years of unfair treatment, Black people demanded equality now. As the crowd gathered around the monument, a young preacher took the stage. This was the first time many people heard Martin Luther King Jr. speak. The audience grew quiet as King called for unity and justice. Soon, the crowd's cheers grew louder as he talked about his dream for America. His voice boomed out, "I have a dream . . ." The people in the crowd nodded their heads in agreement. By the end of his speech, the crowd roared! People around the world heard his powerful speech and saw the crowds calling for justice. The March on Washington and King's words would help change the United States forever.

Martin Luther King Jr. waves to the crowd on August 28, 1963.

CHAPTER 1

EQUAL OPPORTUNITY

In the 1940s, Black people and other people of color were treated unfairly. In many places, Black and white children could not go to the same schools. Most of the U.S. was **segregated**. Good-paying jobs were only for white people. Black people struggled to find jobs that paid enough to support their families. They struggled to find fair housing too. **Discrimination** made things harder for Black people.

In the 1940s, many Black women could only find low-paying jobs, like cleaning houses.

A. Philip Randolph was fed up with what was happening to Black Americans. Randolph was a labor union leader and civil rights **activist**. He was good at organizing people. He led successful strikes and boycotts. His fight for fair employment called for **equal opportunity**. In 1941, Randolph planned to march to Washington, D.C. He would pressure the government to end segregation. He also wanted Congress to allow Black soldiers the same rights as white soldiers. He called it the March on Washington Movement.

A. Philip Randolph proposed a March on Washington in 1941.

President Roosevelt saw that Randolph meant business. Before Randolph could finish planning the **protest**, President Roosevelt made an **executive order**. He created the Fair Employment Practices Committee. It was created to end hiring discrimination. Randolph called the protest off.

President Roosevelt established the Fair Employment Practices Committee in 1941.

Black Americans sitting in protest at a white-only lunch counter in Nashville, Tennessee, in 1960

Years later, Randolph saw that nothing had really changed. Black people were still fighting for equal treatment. Randolph knew it was time for another protest. This time, he wanted something much bigger. He remembered his idea about the March on Washington Movement from the 1940s. Randolph decided to restart plans to march to Washington. He also wanted to include civil rights issues. But he needed support from other leaders. Randolph knew he needed help to gather people from across the nation.

The National Association for the Advancement of Colored People (NAACP) had thousands of members at this time. Randolph knew that he needed to work with NAACP members. They could help him organize a large protest. He also knew that he would need a new face to lead this march. He planned a meeting with a young, popular preacher named Reverend Martin Luther King Jr. to tell him his plan. Randolph had worked with King before. He liked that King also believed in peaceful protests.

The NAACP protesting against school segregation outside an education authority in St. Louis, Missouri

Roy Wilkins (left), Martin Luther King Jr. (center), and
A. Philip Randolph (right) in Washington, D.C., at the
Prayer Pilgrimage for Freedom rally in 1957

CHAPTER 2

TIME TO ORGANIZE

Randolph and his friend Bayard Rustin wanted a large **demonstration**. They wanted to pressure the government to finally create laws that would prevent injustice. They talked to unions, or groups that support workers. They also spoke to civil rights leaders. At first, it was hard for everyone to get together. Each group wanted to make sure their needs were met. Finally, they formed an **alliance**. All the groups agreed that fair treatment was most important. They agreed to work together for one common goal. The alliance would fight for justice together.

Members of different organizations came together to plan the March on Washington.

BIRMINGHAM PROTESTS

In 1963, the Birmingham movement was led by King. It was a nonviolent protest created to bring attention to integration efforts in Birmingham. The nation watched as Black high school students were attacked by police dogs and police holding high-pressure water hoses. The movement helped to change people's attitudes about segregation. The demonstration also laid the foundation for the March on Washington.

In 1963, Walter Gadsden, a high school student, was attacked by a police dog during a civil rights demonstration in Birmingham, Alabama.

Randolph, Rustin, and King were ready to lead the march. Soon, President John F. Kennedy heard about plans for the march. He worried the march would turn violent. The country was still divided by segregation. Protests had turned dangerous in many cities. President Kennedy asked to meet with the organizers. Six organizers of the march met with the president to discuss their plan of nonviolence. After a long meeting, the men agreed that the march would happen. The March on Washington for Jobs and Freedom was underway.

FACT

. . . .

At age 23, John Lewis was the youngest speaker at the March on Washington. In 1986, he was elected to the U.S. House of Representatives.

Civil rights leaders, including Martin Luther King Jr. (first row, third from left), met with Attorney General Robert F. Kennedy (first row, fourth from left) and Vice President Lyndon B. Johnson (first row, second from right) in June 1963.

CHAPTER 3

THE MARCH ON WASHINGTON

The march attracted hundreds of thousands of people. The military and hundreds of extra police were called to monitor the protestors. The strong police presence did not stop the protestors. Hundreds of people rode buses to get to Washington. There were around 250,000 people from different races, religions, and places. They were all there to support civil rights and justice. The crowd gathered at the Washington Monument. It waited for their leaders. King, Rustin, and others spoke to members of Congress before the march. Some of them wanted to attend the event too.

People came from all across the country to attend the March on Washington.

Crowds listened to the speakers on the steps of the Lincoln Memorial.

The March on Washington was so popular that it took over regular TV programming. People across the nation tuned in to hear what King and others had to say. The program featured many speakers and musicians. The speakers supported equality. They talked about change in America. Rustin ended the program by reading a list of demands. The group wanted a fair national minimum wage. They demanded voting rights and immediate desegregation of schools.

NAACP

The NAACP formed in 1909 in response to the ongoing violence against Black people in the United States. The group's mission is to ensure that people have equal rights. When the NAACP was formed, the term *colored people* was used to describe Black people and was included in the group's name. Today, this term is offensive to Black people.

A 1949 NAACP poster calling people to join the organization

CHAPTER 4

HISTORY IS MADE

The march was a positive statement. It attracted many people who wanted justice in America. One of the most famous moments of the day was King's "I Have a Dream" speech. King had prepared a speech about civil rights. In the middle of his speech, he changed it. His good friend Mahalia Jackson inspired him to talk about his dream. He spoke about his dream for his children. He also talked about a world in which everyone would be treated fairly.

The crowd watched speeches at the Lincoln Memorial.

Gospel singer Mahalia Jackson sang in front of the crowd right before Martin Luther King Jr.'s speech.

Martin Luther King Jr. gave his famous "I Have a Dream" speech from the steps of the Lincoln Memorial.

The world listened to his powerful words. King had been in the news for leading protests. He had even been arrested for **civil disobedience**. Although he was a peaceful protestor, many white people considered King trouble during the 1960s. This was because he spoke out against injustice, even if it made people angry or uncomfortable. In reality, King was a strong leader and voice for change. King delivered a clear message of hope and equality. He soon became the face of the Civil Rights Movement.

FACT

Daisy Bates was an activist from Arkansas and a leader in the NAACP. She was the only woman to speak during the program at the March on Washington.

CHAPTER 5

THE DREAM

The March on Washington brought awareness to the fight for civil rights. It was shown in many households across the nation. The call for equality and justice was heard around the world. The march was a step forward, but change was still far away. About a month later, a church was bombed in Alabama. The blast killed four young Black girls. The nation was horrified that innocent children were killed. It was not until June 19, 1964, that Congress passed the Civil Rights Act. This act made discrimination illegal. It allowed Black people and other people of color to finally have the same rights as other Americans.

People protested after four Black girls were killed in a church bombing in Birmingham, Alabama.

President Johnson signing the 1964 Civil Rights Act as Martin Luther King Jr. and others look on

The March on Washington is one of the most important protests in American history. The march focused on civil rights and jobs at a time when Black people were fighting for equality. Martin Luther King Jr. told the world about his dream. He hoped that the world would see his vision of equality for all. The fight against injustice continues. King's message of equality and justice rings true to those who still work toward fulfilling his dream.

FACT

On August 28, 2020, the NAACP held an event to recommit to Dr. King's dream. Due to the COVID-19 pandemic, the march was a virtual event.

The March on Washington was the largest civil rights event ever held at the time.